THE RENAL SLOW COOKER COOKBOOK

50 Delicious & Hearty Renal Diet Recipes That Practically Cook Themselves

CARRILLO PRESS

CARRILLO PRESS

Contents

INTRODUCTION

Welcome to The Renal Slow Cooker Cookbook!

The second in the collection of Renal Diet Cookbooks from Carillo Press, the Slow Cooker Cookbook is created to make your life a little easier with 50 slow cooker recipes suitable for the renal diet.

We understand that finding out that you or a loved one has kidney disease is a tough and probably stressful time, not only for the sufferer but for those around them too. Now you know that not only your lifestyle but your diet and eating habits will have to change too. Whether you or someone you know has been diagnosed, you think you may be suffering from the symptoms but are not sure, or if you have a family history of chronic kidney disease and want to find out more about it as well as what you can do to possibly prevent it getting to the later stages, this book provides information about the possible causes, symptoms and dietary needs of kidney disease. It is always absolutely vital that you use this information alongside professional guidance; make sure you see your doctor if you are experiencing, or suspect you may be experiencing, kidney disease, It is also essential you continue to see your doctor, nutritionist or nephrologist regularly after your diagnosis and consult them before you make any dietary or lifestyle changes.

As well as an overview of the disease, its causes and symptoms, this book provides you with information about different foods you can continue to eat and those you should cut down or avoid altogether. As well as this, the specific nutrients and minerals that you need to be aware of are outlined (sodium, potassium and phosphorous) along with recommended levels that you should be adhering to each day. Again, this must be confirmed by your doctor, as these depend on a number of factors including age, gender, weight and the stage of kidney disease you're experiencing.

The good news is that with the right diet, medication and lifestyle, it is possible to delay and even prevent the need for dialysis and kidney transplants. The rest of this book is dedicated to providing you with healthy and delicious recipes that can be prepared in the slow cooker, leaving you time to do the things you enjoy! The nutritional values of each dish is given so you can plan and prepare easily and then simply enjoy delicious meals after the slow cooker does the hard work!

We wish you all the best in the kitchen and in health!

C1: THE TRUTH ABOUT KIDNEY DISEASE

Our kidneys perform vital functions in our body to help keep us healthy; they help to maintain mineral levels such as potassium, sodium and phosphorous, as well as regulate water levels. The kidneys also remove waste and extra fluids from our body after digestion, muscle activity or from exposure to certain medications and chemicals.

The enzyme renin, secreted by the kidneys, helps to regulate blood pressure and create erythropoietin, the hormone that helps trigger the formation of red blood cells by bone marrow. These are both vital for healthy functioning. Last but not least, our kidneys generate an active vitamin D that we need for healthy bones. If left untreated, kidney disease could lead to kidney failure. Treatment for kidney failure is usually dialysis or a kidney transplant. However, kidney disease can be slowed down and treated with the right balance of medication, nutrition and advice from your professional consultant.

If you experience kidney disease for longer than three months and it goes untreated then you will develop chronic kidney disease. Often, the symptoms of kidney disease can go unnoticed and therefore this can be dangerous as some patients develop chronic kidney disease without even being aware that they have experienced the earlier stages.

Causes of Kidney Disease

High blood pressure and diabetes (both type 1 and type 2) are the top two causes of kidney disease. However, if you do have diabetes, this can be controlled by monitoring blood sugar levels in order to help to prevent kidney disease as well as coronary heart disease and strokes.

Other causes include:

- Immune system diseases such as lupus, hepatitis B and C, and HIV,
- Frequent urinary tract infections affecting your kidneys (pyelonephritis) could cause scars to build up which can lead to damage of the kidneys,
- Inflammation of the glomeruli (the tiny filters inside the kidneys) can occur

after strep infections,
- An inherited kidney disease called polycystic kidney disease causes fluid filled cysts to form in the kidneys,
- NSAIDS drugs such as naproxen and ibuprofen used for a prolonged period of time can permanently damage the kidneys,
- Taking illegal drugs such as heroin,
- Long-term exposure to certain chemicals can cause the breakdown of kidney functions.

Acute Renal Failure

If you experience a sudden, total loss of kidney function, this is known as acute renal failure. There are three top causes of renal failure:

1. Lack of blood reaching the kidneys,
2. Urine not being expelled from the kidneys,
3. Direct damage to the kidneys.

There are several factors that can cause these three things to happen including:

- Traumatic injuries causing severe blood loss,
- Sepsis (an infection that can cause the body to go into shock),
- Severe dehydration (particularly in athletes because of the sudden breakdown of muscles and the release of large amounts of a protein called myoglobin that causes harm to the kidneys),
- An enlarged prostate,
- Drug/toxins,
- Eclampsia/pre-eclampsia/HELLP Syndrome in pregnant women.

Symptoms of Kidney Disease

There are many different symptoms that you may experience with kidney disease and these include:

- Fatigue,
- Loss of appetite,
- Difficulty concentrating,
- Sleep problems,
- Needing to urinate more frequently,
- Blood in urine,
- Foamy urine,
- Muscle cramps or twitches,
- Swelling in the ankles or feet (edema),
- Dry or itchy skin,
- Puffiness around your eyes.

Experiencing one or more of these symptoms may be an indication that you have kidney disease and you should consult a professional if you do experience any of the above. As these symptoms may also be a result of another illness or disease, kidney disease can often go unnoticed. It is even more important you ask your doctor about kidney disease if you do suffer from diabetes, high blood pressure, if you have a family history of kidney disease, or are over 60 years old.

Symptoms of acute renal failure include:

- Shortness of breath due to fluid build up,
- Reduced amount of urine,
- Ongoing nausea,
- Weakness,
- A pain or intense pressure on your chest.

Remember the only way of knowing you have kidney disease at any stage is through consulting a professional who will conduct a urinalysis, measure urine volume, take blood samples or use ultrasound to diagnose you. It is vital once you have been diagnosed that you follow the professional advice given to you, in order to prevent kidney failure. This will usually involve a combination of medication; a healthy lifestyle; a reduction of over-the-counter medications such as aspirin; as well as toxins in the home such as tobacco and cleaning products.

Five Stages of Kidney Disease

The different stages of kidney disease are determined by the Glomerular Filtration Rate (GFR). This is the process where the kidneys filter the blood that removes fluids and wastes. The GFR calculation determines how well the blood is being filtered.

The GFR is calculated using a formula that includes your age, race, gender, and serum creatinine levels. The lower the number, the further along your kidney disease will be. As always, this would have to be monitored and diagnosed by a professional.

Stage 1 kidney disease: GFR = approximately 90+

At this stage, you may not have any symptoms and so this is why it is often unnoticed. If your doctor does determine you have Stage 1 chronic kidney disease (CKD) it will usually be due to diabetes or high blood pressure. If there is a family history of polycystic kidney disease, you have a greater chance of experiencing chronic kidney disease. Therefore it is wise to go for check ups in order to ensure you do not have kidney disease, especially if you also suffer from any of the symptoms in the previous section.
Treatments: if diagnosed at this stage your doctor or nephrologist will recommend suitable treatment including medication and a healthy diet and lifestyle. The goal is to keep the kidneys functioning healthily on their own for as long as possible and to potentially avoid having to go through dialysis or a kidney transplant.

Stage 2 kidney disease: GFR = 60-89

Symptoms in stage 2 might include higher levels of urea or creatinine in your blood; there may be protein or blood in your urine.
Treatment as above for stage 1 kidney disease.

Stage 3 kidney disease: 3a GFR = 45-59
3b GFR = 30-44

This stage is classed as moderate kidney damage. Waste products will start to collect in the blood, which can cause uremia as the kidney function declines. This makes it more likely for you to develop kidney disease complications such as bone disease, anaemia, red blood cell shortage, or high blood pressure.
At this stage you may start to experience kidney pain in your lower back as well as sleep problems due to cramps in your legs. Fatigue is more common at this stage, along with swelling of extremities or edema, shortness of breath, and fluid retention. You might notice changes in your urine such as a foamy consistency or changes in color to red, tea-colored, dark orange, or brown. Urination frequency may change.

Treatments: As Stage 3 kidney disease progresses it is recommended that you see a nephrologist who will perform a number of tests on your kidneys; you may also be sent to a dietician to help with your nutrition and meal plans.
If you have high blood pressure, your doctor will likely prescribe medicine. ACE inhibitors and angiotensin receptor blockers have shown the potential to slow down kidney disease progression in people who don't suffer from high blood pressure. You should ask your doctor about your medications and take them only as prescribed. You need to make sure you are taking your medicines, eating healthily, not smoking and exercising regularly to help prolong your kidney function. Talk with your doctor about an exercise plan; your doctor can also help you stop smoking. Kidney disease can't be cured but by following your doctor's advice and guidance you can slow down its progress.

Stage 4 kidney disease: GFR = 15-30

At this stage, waste collects in the blood causing uremia as kidney function decreases. Complications such as high blood pressure, cardiovascular disease, heart disease, anaemia, and bone disease are likely to develop.

Treatments:
Appointments with your nephrologist are essential at least once every

three months. They will conduct tests for creatinine, calcium, phosphorus, and haemoglobin levels to ascertain how well the kidneys are functioning. They will also monitor your blood pressure and diabetes if applicable. The ultimate goal is to keep your kidneys functioning for as long as possible but it is also possible that they may start to prepare your body for dialysis.

There are two main forms of dialysis:
Hemodialysis can be conducted either at a centre or in your home by a care partner. The dialysis machine will remove some of your blood through an artificial kidney or dialyzer to clean out the toxins that your kidneys can't remove by themselves any more. The cleaned blood is then returned to your body.
Peritoneal dialysis is needle free and you don't need anyone to assist you.
The last option would be to have a kidney transplant.

Stage 5 kidney disease: GFR = 15 or below

This is end stage kidney disease. The kidneys will have lost all function and will not be able to work effectively. You will need a kidney transplant or dialysis to survive. With stage 5 kidney disease you might experience increased skin pigmentation; tingling of your hands or feet; muscle cramps; swelling around your eyes or ankles; little or no urine flow; unexplained itching; problems concentrating; and fatigue. You may well start feeling better once you begin dialysis. By removing the toxins from the blood and replacing the functions with medicine you could enjoy a fairly good quality of life.
If a kidney transplant is recommended or desired, your nephrologist will explain the process to you and get your name on a waiting list for a donated kidney or help you find a living donor.

C2: RENAL DIET AND NUTRITION

How Can Diet Affect Symptoms of Kidney Disease?

Changing your diet and lifestyle can go a long way in helping to control your kidney disease and prevent the later stages of kidney disease. This chapter will explore the different food and nutrient groups that you should familiarise yourself with if you have kidney disease. Please always consult your doctor before making changes to your diet.

Carbohydrates - should make up the majority of your diet, as they're the primary source of energy for your body.
There are two types of carbohydrates: complex and simple. An example of a simple carbohydrate is fruit. Fruit is packed with the fiber, vitamins and energy that your body needs. Examples of complex carbohydrates are grains, breads, and vegetables. All these carbohydrates provide minerals and vitamins as well as energy and fiber. Carbohydrates also play a vital role in balancing blood-sugar levels.

Protein - repairs tissue and builds muscle. Your body also uses protein to build antibodies. These are your body's defence against disease. Animal foods are the primary sources of protein such as milk, beef, eggs, chicken and pork. Protein can also be found in some plants. Legumes, nuts, and soy bean products are all good sources of proteins. Vegetables also contain small amounts of protein. Protein is essential for good health however in later stages of chronic kidney disease your renal dietitian may have you cut back on protein intake to help reduce stress on the kidneys.

Fats- transport vitamins K, E, D, and A to your cells. They produce the hormones testosterone and estrogen. Some fats contain fatty acids that are good for your skin. These fatty acids also make up linings of cells in the body and help with the transmission of nerves. However, too much fat or the wrong kind of fat in your diet can cause weight gain, leading to heart disease and many other problems with your health.

There are two types of fats: unsaturated and saturated. Meat and dairy products are saturated fats. Too much of these fats can elevate your cholesterol; this cholesterol is what causes heart disease and clogged arteries. The food and drug administration recommend reducing your saturated fat intake. Nuts, fish, and certain oils are good sources of unsaturated fats and all help to reduce cholesterol. Trans fats will raise cholesterol levels just like saturated fats. The FDA suggests you choose food that is low in trans fats and saturated fats. Processed foods usually contain trans fats.

Sodium, potassium, and phosphorus - are the three main minerals balanced by the kidneys. As chronic kidney disease gets worse, some foods will need to be avoided as your kidneys will no longer be able to get rid of the excess from these minerals. Blood tests will be conducted to monitor the levels of these minerals.

Sodium -In the early stages of kidney disease, a low sodium diet may be all you need if you have high blood pressure. Your kidneys cannot get rid of excess fluid and sodium from your body whilst experiencing kidney disease. To help identify salt in foods look for ingredients on the label such as baking powder, sodium or brine. Generally, children and adults should eat less than 2,300 mg of sodium a day.
Kidney disease stage 1 and 2 = 1-3.5g per day
Kidney disease stage 3 - 4 = 1-2.5g per day
Kidney disease stage 5 = 1-2g per day

Potassium -Kidneys usually get rid of excess potassium in your urine to maintain normal levels in your blood. When experiencing kidney disease they can no longer do this effectively.
Hyperkalemia (or high potassium levels) occurs in the later stages of kidney disease. Symptoms of high potassium are a slow pulse, numbness, weakness, and nausea.
Kidney disease stage 1 and 2 = 2-5g per day
Kidney disease stage 3 - 4 =2-4g per day
Kidney disease stage 5 = 2-2.5per day

Phosphorus - Since your kidneys can no longer remove phosphorus from your blood and urine, hyperphosphatemia or high phosphorus may become a problem during stage 4 or 5 kidney disease.

Kidney disease stage 1 and 2 = up to 1000mg per day
Kidney disease stage 3 - 4 (GFR of 25-90+)= p to 1000mg per day
Kidney disease stage 4 (GFR of 15-25) = up to 750mgper day
Kidney disease stage 4 (GFR of 5-15) = up to 7mg per kg of body weight
(Capicchiano, 2017)

C3 -RENAL DIET AND LIFESTYLE GUIDANCE

1. Always follow your dietician's advice in conjunction with any research or cookbooks you use: During kidney disease this is extremely important. They can advise you about sodium, phosphorous and potassium content of favorite foods and give you recommendations on how to reduce your sodium intake. Your diet will be tailored to you, taking into account the stage of kidney disease you're in and any other illnesses or diseases you suffer from.

2. Keep a Food Diary: You should track what you're eating and drinking in order to stay within the guidelines and recommendations given to you. Apps such as My Fitness Pal make this extremely easy and even track many of the minerals and levels in foods including sodium, protein etc. There are also apps specifically made for kidney disease patients to track sodium, phosphorous and potassium levels.

3. Read Food Labels: Some foods have hidden sodium in them, even if they don't taste salty. You will need to cut back on the amount of canned, frozen, and processed foods you eat. Check your beverages for added sodium.
Check food labels to avoid: Potassium chloride, Tetrasodium phosphate, Sodium phosphate, Trisodium phosphate, Tricalcium phosphate, Phosphoric acid, Polyphosphate, Hexametaphosphate, Pyrophosphate, Monocalcium phosphate, Dicalcium phosphate, Aluminum phosphate, Sodium tripolyphosphate, Sodium polyphosphate.

4. Flavor foods with fresh herbs and spices instead of shop-bought dressings and condiments: These add flavor and variety to your meals and are not packed with sodium; spices also have many health benefits! Also stay away from salt substitutes and seasonings that contain potassium. Use citrus fruits and vinegars for dressings and to add flavor.

5: Keep Up Your Appointments With Your Doctor or Nephrologist:
Let your doctor know if you notice any swelling or changes in your weight.

6. Monitor drink and fluid intake: You have probably been told you need to drink up to eight glasses of water a day. This is true for a healthy body but for people experiencing the later stages of CKD, these fluids can build up and cause additional problems. The restriction of fluids will differ from person to person. Things to take into consideration are swelling, urine output, and weight gain. Your weight will be recorded before dialysis begins and once it's over. This is done to determine how much fluid to remove from your body. If you are undergoing haemodialysis, this will be recorded approximately three times a week. If you are undergoing peritoneal dialysis, your weight is recorded every day. If there is a significant weight gain you may be drinking too many fluids.

7. Measure portion sizes -Moderating your portion sizes is essential. Use smaller cups, bowls, or plates to avoid giving yourself oversized portions.
Measure your food so you can keep an accurate record of how much you are actually eating:

The size of your fist is equal to 1 cup.
The palm of your hand is equal to 3 ounces.
The tip of your thumb is equivalent to 1 teaspoon.
A poker chip is equal to 1 tablespoon.

Substitution Tips:
- Use plain white flour instead of whole-wheat/whole-grain
- Use all-purpose flour instead of self-raising,
- Use Stevia instead of sugar,
- Use egg whites rather than whole eggs,
- Use almond rice or soy milk instead of cows milk.

8. Other Advice: Be careful when eating in restaurants -ask for dressings and condiments on the side and watch out for soups and cured meats.
Watch out for convenience foods that are high in sodium.
Prepare your own meals and freeze them for later use.
Drain liquids from canned vegetables and fruits to help control potassium levels.

Foods to Avoid:

- Cured meats
- Bacon and ham
- Cold cuts
- Frozen dinners
- Salted nuts
- Canned beans with salt added
- Canned entrées
- Raisins
- Oranges
- Cantaloupe
- Pumpkin
- Potatoes
- Dried beans
- Tomatoes
- Yogurt
- Ice Cream
- Milk
- Nuts and seeds
- Salt substitutes
- Molasses
- Chocolate
- Bottled coffee drinks
- Non-dairy creamers
- Cereal bars
- Enhanced chicken and meat
- Sodas
- Iced teas
- Flavored waters
- Sardines
- Offal
- Processed meats
- Dried beans
- Nuts and nut butters
- Avocado
- Pizza
- Biscuits, pancakes, waffles

- Corn tortillas
- Whole grain crackers, breads, cereals
- Bran
- Beer, chocolate drinks, cola, milk-based coffee
- Cheese
- Salted Butter
- Coconut
- Solid shortening

High potassium fruits should be avoided. A serving of the following listed fruits has more than 250 mg of potassium:

- 5 dried prunes or ½ cup prune juice
- 1/8 of a honeydew melon
- ¼ cup dates
- ½ cup orange juice or 1 small orange
- 1 small nectarine no bigger than 2 inches across

These vegetables have more than 250 mg of potassium in each 1.2 cup serving.

- Fresh beets
- Winter squash
- Tomatoes, juice, or ¼ cup sauce
- Sweet potatoes
- Potatoes
- Okra and Brussel sprouts
- ¼ avocado or 1 whole artichoke

Foods To Enjoy:

Red bell peppers have low potassium but lots of flavor. They are also a good way to get folic acid, fiber, vitamin C, A, and B6. Red bell peppers also contain lycopene - an antioxidant that helps protect against cancer. A ½ cup serving contains 10 mg of phosphorus, 88 mg of potassium and 1 mg of sodium.

Cabbage contains phytochemicals - a chemical compound found in fruits and vegetables that helps break up free radicals. Phytochemicals are known to protect against cancer and help keep your heart healthy. Cabbage is high in vitamin C, K, B6, folic acid and fiber. A ½ cup serving contains just 9 mg of phosphorus, 60 mg potassium, and 6 mg sodium.

Cauliflower contains indoles, glucosinolates, and thiocyanates. These help the liver get rid of toxins that could damage cell membrane and DNA. A ½ cup serving of boiled cauliflower has 20 mg phosphorus, 88 mg potassium, 9 mg sodium. Garlic helps reduce inflammation, keeps plaque from building on your teeth, and lowers cholesterol. Just one clove of garlic has 4 mg of phosphorus, 12 mg of potassium and 1 mg of sodium.

Onion contains quercetin an antioxidant that protects against cancers and helps heart disease. Onions contain chromium - a mineral that helps with protein, carbohydrate and fat metabolism. A ½ cup serving has 3 mg phosphorus, 116 mg potassium, and 3 mg sodium.

Apples prevent constipation, reduce cholesterol, reduce the risk of cancer, and protects against heart disease. Apples have anti-inflammatory compounds and are high in fiber. Just 1 medium apple with skin on has no sodium, 158 mg of potassium and 10 mg of phosphorus.

Cranberries can keep you from getting a bladder infection because they prevent bacteria from sticking to the bladder wall. Cranberries can also help the stomach from creating the bacteria that causes ulcers thus promoting good GI health. Cranberries can also protect against heart disease and cancer. A ½ cup cranberry juice cocktail has 3 mg phosphorus, 22 mg potassium, 3 mg sodium. A ¼ cup of cranberry sauce has 6 mg phosphorus, 17 mg potassium, and 35 mg sodium. A ½ cup of dried cranberries has 5 mg phosphorus, 24 mg potassium, and 2 mg sodium.

Blueberries help reduce inflammation. Blueberries contain manganese, fiber, and vitamin C. They also help protect the brain from the effects of aging. A ½ cup of fresh blueberries has 7 mg phosphorus, 65 mg potassium, and 4 mg sodium.

Raspberries contain phytonutrient ellagic acid which helps reduce free radical cell damage. They are high in vitamin C, manganese, folate, and fibre. A ½ cup of raspberries has 7 mg phosphorus, 93 mg potassium, 0 mg sodium.

Strawberries are a good source of manganese, vitamin C, and fibre. They provide anti-inflammatory and anti-cancer compounds and help to protect the heart. A ½ cup or 13 mg phosphorus, 120 mg potassium, 1 mg sodium.

Cherries, when eaten daily, can help reduce inflammation.. A ½ cup serving of fresh cherries has 15 mg phosphorus, 160 mg potassium, 0 mg sodium.

Red grapes protect against heart disease by reducing blood clots. They also help protect against inflammation and cancer. A ½ cup red grapes has 4 mg phosphorus, 88 mg potassium, 1 mg sodium.

Egg whites contain the highest quality protein and essential amino acids. 2 egg whites contain 10 mg phosphorus, 108 mg potassium, 110 mg sodium, and 7 grams protein.

Fish is a source of protein and anti-inflammatory fats known as omega-3s. Omega-3s help fight heart disease and cancer. It is recommended that you eat fish two times a week.

Olive oil helps fight against oxidation and inflammation. Virgin olive oils contain more antioxidants. 1 tablespoon olive oil serving contains less than 0 mg of phosphorus, less than a mg of potassium, and 1 mg of sodium.

Vitamins and minerals: Our bodies need vitamins to be able to function correctly. The best way to achieve this is make sure you eat a well-rounded diet. However, if you have chronic kidney disease, you may not be able to get all the recommended vitamins through diet alone. Vitamins that are usually recommended by your renal dietitian are vitamin C, biotin, pantothenic acid, niacin, vitamin B12, B6, B2, B1, and folic acid. You must consult your doctor or dietician before starting to take vitamin supplements.

C4: EATING OUT AND SHOPPING ON A RENAL DIET

Advice for Dining Out:

You don't have to miss out on your favorite restaurant or cuisines! Follow these tips to stay healthy:
- Look out for small or half portions and ask your server for your foods to be cooked without extra salts, butters or sauces.
- Avoid fried foods and opt for grilled or poached instead.
- If you know you are going out to eat, plan ahead: look at the restaurant's menu beforehand and decide what you will order to avoid anxiety or stress on the night!
- Use the food lists in the previous chapter to help you choose and don't feel bad about asking them to cater for your needs.
- Be sure to take your phosphorus binders, if they have been prescribed to you. Take them with your meal instead of waiting until you get home.

Advice for traveling:

Whatever your travel plans, you will have to eat.
- If you plan ahead, you should be able to make a meal plan with your renal dietitian.
- Tell your dietitian where you are going and what you expect to eat at your destination.
- Remember to pack any prescriptions you may have such as phosphate binders.
- If you are diabetic remember to keep carbohydrate intake to a minimum.
- Try not to eat sweets such as sweetened drinks, fruit juices, cakes, pies, and candy.
- Don't consume salty foods like chips, crackers, and pretzels.
- Limit condiments such as soy sauce, salad dressing, and ketchup. Keep a check on your blood sugar daily.

- If going on a road trip or camping, avoid processed meats. If at all possible, use fresh-cooked meats, low-sodium deli meats, unsalted chicken or tuna.
- Choose unsalted pretzels or crackers instead of potato chips. Salty foods need to be avoided if you are on a fluid restricted diet.
- Take along nutritional drinks formulated for kidney patients. These can always be used as a meal replacement if need be.
- Remember to check labels for sodium content.
- Do not consume dairy products unless they are allowed as part of your diet plan.
- If you are going on a cruise, all those buffet foods are tempting to eat 24 hours a day. To help with this predicament try to select fruits, salads, and vegetables from the lists in the previous chapter.
- Remember to include a good source of protein with every meal and avoid breads and sauces that are salty. You could pack you own snacks to eat between meals.
- Let the cruise line know of your dietary needs, most are willing to prepare special foods for you. Low-sodium meal options may also be available.
- If you are going to be traveling abroad and don't speak the language, bring a phrasebook that has a section for ordering food.

Cooking Tips:

1. Grill, poach, roast or sauté meats instead of frying.
2. Steam or boil vegetables instead of frying.
3. Use healthy oils such as extra virgin olive oil to shallow fry.
4. Soak fruit and vegetables in warm water for 2 hours before cooking in order to reduce potassium levels – especially potatoes!
5. When using canned beans and vegetables, make sure to rinse and drain them.
6. Drain liquid from canned or frozen vegetables and fruits.

One Last Thing:

Always remember to use new recipes and ingredients after speaking to your doctor or dietitian; your needs will be unique to you depending on the stage of chronic kidney disease you're experiencing. We hope that with your doctor's advice, along with our guidance and recipes, that you can continue to enjoy cooking, eating and sharing meal times with your love ones.

BREAKFAST

Easy Morning Slow Cooked Oats

SERVES 4 / PREP TIME: 5 MINUTES / COOK TIME: 7-8 HOURS

A brilliant bowl of energy to keep you up and running until lunch.

1 cup of jumbo oats
4 cups of almond milk (unenriched)
1 tsp. of ground cinnamon
To serve: 1 cup of raspberries

1. Heat your slow cooker.
2. Find a sturdy ceramic bowl that fits nicely in the cooker.
3. Put the oats in the bowl and pour the milk on top.
4. Sprinkle in the cinnamon.
5. Place the bowl in the slow cooker on its lowest setting
6. Cook overnight for 7-8 hours.
7. To serve, stir and add a drop more milk or water to your desired consistency.
8. Add the raspberries on top and enjoy.

Per Serving: Calories: 187
- Protein: 4g
- Carbohydrates: 33g
- Fat: 4g
- Cholesterol: 0mg
- Sodium: 159mg
- Potassium: 247mg
- Phosphorus: 112mg
- Calcium: 484mg
- Fiber: 5g

Soft and Spicy Vegetarian Enchiladas

SERVES 4 / PREP TIME: 10 MINUTES / COOK TIME: 2-3 HOURS

These soft and zingy enchiladas are filling, nutritious and great for sharing.

4 whole wheat tortillas
2 large egg whites
1 ½ cups of almond milk (unenriched)
(Optional) 1 red chili, de-seeded and finely chopped
1 yellow bell pepper, chopped
¾ cup of sliced scallions

2 tbsp. of chopped fresh cilantro
1 tbsp. of finely chopped chives
1 cup of frozen peas

1. Spray the inside of your slow cooker with cooking spray.
2. Place two of the tortillas in the bottom of the slow cooker.
3. Using a fork beat the egg whites, milk and chili in a small bowl.
4. Keep 2 tbsp. of chopped bell pepper and 2 tbsp. of scallions set aside for later.
5. Tip the remaining bell pepper and scallions onto the tortillas.
6. Use the final two tortillas to cover it all up.
7. Pour the egg mixture over the top.
8. Cover with foil or baking paper and cook on a Low heat setting for 4 to 5 hours or on High heat setting 2 to 3 hours or until the center is set.
9. Sprinkle with the rest of the bell pepper, scallions, cilantro and chives.
10. Remove the foil before serving by loosening the edges with a knife.

Per Serving: Calories: 180
Protein: 8g
Carbohydrates: 28g
Fat: 4g
Cholesterol: 0mg
Sodium: 293mg
Potassium: 309mg
Phosphorus: 173mg
Calcium: 201mg
Fiber: 7g

Light and Fluffy Frittata

SERVES 4 / PREP TIME: 10 MINUTES / COOK TIME: 4-5 HOURS

Light, healthy and full of flavor. Serve as a side or with a generous salad helping.

1 tsp. olive oil
1 cup of baby spinach
1 red bell pepper, finely diced
¼ cup of green onions, sliced
¼ cup of brie (optional, broken into small pieces)
1 tsp. of basil
3 large egg whites
1 tsp. of black pepper

1. Wash the spinach in a colander and pat it dry with a paper towel.
2. Lightly oil the inside of the slow cooker.
3. Add the red pepper, green onions and baby spinach to the cooker.
4. Beat the eggs vigorously with a fork and stir in the basil.
5. Pour in the mix and stir.
6. Sprinkle on the brie (optional).
7. Cook on the lowest setting for 1-2 hours or until the frittata is set and the brie is melted.
8. Serve hot.

Per Serving: Calories: 66
Protein: 5g
Carbohydrates: 3g
Fat: 4g
Cholesterol: 9mg
Sodium: 144mg
Potassium: 184mg
Phosphorus: 35mg
Calcium: 35mg
Fiber: 1g

Creamy Buckwheat and Plum Porridge

SERVES 8 / PREP TIME: 5 MINUTES / COOK TIME: 4-5 HOURS

Smooth, warm and sweet with notes of spice.

---

5 cups of almond milk (un-enriched)
1 ½ cups buckwheat groats
2 tbsp. ground cinnamon
1 cup of plums, pitted and sliced

---

1. Add the almond milk to the slow cooker.
2. Pour in the buckwheat, cinnamon and sliced plum pieces.
3. Cook gently overnight on the lowest setting for 6-10 hours.
4. It's that simple!

Per Serving: Calories: 163
Protein: 4g
Carbohydrates: 34g
Fat: 2g
Cholesterol: 0mg
Sodium: 101mg
Potassium: 207mg
Phosphorus: 84mg
Calcium: 316mg
Fiber: 4g

Golden Broccoli Frittata

SERVES 12 / PREP TIME: 10 MINUTES / COOK TIME: 5 -7 HOURS

This frittata is hearty and delicious with a little bit of kick.

---

4 large egg whites
½ cup of coconut milk (unenriched)
1 tsp. of Dijon mustard
1 cup of scallions, chopped

½ tsp. of black pepper
1 head of broccoli, finely chopped
1 small white onion, diced
2 carrots, grated

---

1. Lightly oil your slow cooker with a little cooking spray.
2. Lightly beat together the egg whites, milk, dry mustard, scallions and pepper.
3. Place 1/3 of the broccoli in an even layer in the slow cooker.
4. Top with 1/3 of the onion and ½ of the carrot.
5. Repeat the layers two more times.
6. Pour the egg mixture over the top.
7. Cook on Low for 5-7 hours, or until eggs are set and the top is golden brown.
8. Share and serve with a crisp green salad.

Per Serving: Calories: 54
Protein: 3g
Carbohydrates: 6g
Fat: 3g
Cholesterol: 0mg
Sodium: 70mg
Potassium: 249mg
Phosphorus: 54mg
Calcium: 34mg
Fiber: 3g

MEAT

Mouthwatering Beef and Chilli Stew

SERVES 6 / PREP TIME: 15 MINUTES / COOK TIME: 7 HOURS

This is a rich, steaming stew with tender beef and sweet spices.

1/2 medium red onion, thinly sliced into half moons
1/2 tbsp. vegetable oil
10oz of flat cut beef brisket, whole
½ cup low sodium stock
¾ cup water
½ tbsp. honey

½ tbsp. chili powder
½ tsp. smoked paprika
½ tsp. dried thyme
1 tsp. black pepper
1 tbsp. corn starch

---

1. Throw the sliced onion into the slow cooker first.
2. Add a splash of oil to a large hot skillet and briefly seal the beef on all sides.
3. Remove the beef from skillet and place in the slow cooker.
4. Add the stock, water, honey and spices to the same skillet that you cooked the beef in.
5. Loosen the browned bits from bottom of pan with spatula. (Hint: These brown bits at the bottom are called the fond.)
6. Allow juice to simmer until the volume is reduced by about half.
7. Pour the juice over beef in the slow cooker.
8. Set slow cooker on Low and cook for approximately 7 hours.
9. Take the beef out of the slow cooker and onto a platter.
10. Shred it with two forks.
11. Pour the remaining juice into a medium saucepan. Bring to a simmer.
12. Whisk the cornstarch with two tbsp. of water.
13. Add to the juice and cook until slightly thickened.
14. For a thicker sauce, simmer and reduce the juice a bit more before adding cornstarch.
15. Pour the sauce over the meat and serve.

Per Serving: Calories: 128
Protein: 13g
Carbohydrates: 6g
Fat: 6g
Cholesterol: 39mg
Sodium: 228mg
Potassium: 202mg
Phosphorus: 119mg
Calcium: 16mg
Fiber: 1g

Beef and Three Pepper Stew

SERVES 6 / PREP TIME: 15 MINUTES / COOK TIME: 6 HOURS

Colorful and delicious, and perfect with a nice crusty white bread.

10oz of flat cut beef brisket, whole
1 tsp. of dried thyme
1 tsp. of black pepper
1 clove garlic
½ cup of green onion, thinly sliced
½ cup low sodium chicken stock
2 cups water

1 large green bell pepper, sliced
1 large red bell pepper, sliced
1 large yellow bell pepper, sliced
1 large red onion, sliced

---

1. Combine the beef, thyme, pepper, garlic, green onion, stock and water in a slow cooker.
2. Leave it all to cook on High for 4-5 hours until tender.
3. Remove the beef from the slow cooker and let it cool.
4. Shred the beef with two forks and remove any excess fat.
5. Place the shredded beef back into the slow cooker.
6. Add the sliced peppers and the onion.
7. Cook on High for 45 to 60 minutes until the vegetables are tender.

Per Serving: Calories: 132
Protein: 14g
Carbohydrates: 9g
Fat: 5g
Cholesterol: 39mg
Sodium: 179mg
Potassium: 390mg
Phosphorus: 141mg
Calcium: 33mg
Fiber: 2g

Sticky Pulled Beef Open Sandwiches

SERVES 5 / PREP TIME: 15 MINUTES / COOK TIME: 5 HOURS

These make a brilliant treat for barbecues with a rich, smoky taste.

½ cup of green onion, sliced
2 garlic cloves
2 tbsp. of fresh parsley
2 large carrots
7oz of flat cut beef brisket, whole
1 tbsp. of smoked paprika
1 tsp. dried parsley
1 tsp. of brown sugar
½ tsp. of black pepper
2 tbsp. of olive oil
¼ cup of red wine

8 tbsp. of cider vinegar
3 cups of water
5 slices white bread
1 cup of arugula to garnish

---

1. Finely chop the green onion, garlic and fresh parsley.
2. Grate the carrot.
3. Put the beef in to roast in a slow cooker.
4. Add the chopped onion, garlic and remaining ingredients, leaving the rolls, fresh parsley and arugula to one side.
5. Stir in the slow cooker to combine.
6. Cover and cook on Low for 8 to 10 hours, or on High for 4 to 5 hours until tender. (Hint: Test for tenderness by pressing into the meat with a fork.)
7. Remove the meat from the slow cooker.
8. Shred it apart with two forks.
9. Return the meat to the broth to keep it warm until ready to serve.
10. Lightly toast the bread and top with shredded beef, arugula, fresh parsley and ½ spoon of the broth.
11. Serve.

Per Serving: Calories: 273
Protein: 15g
Carbohydrates: 20g
Fat: 11g
Cholesterol: 37mg
Sodium: 308mg
Potassium: 399mg
Phosphorus: 159mg
Calcium: 113mg
Fiber: 3g

Herby Beef Stroganoff and Fluffy Rice

SERVES 6 / PREP TIME: 15 MINUTES / COOK TIME: 5 HOURS

This dish is rich and indulgent with aromatic herbs.

½ cup onion
2 garlic cloves
9oz of flat cut beef brisket, cut into 1"
cubes
½ cup of reduced-sodium beef stock
1/3 cup red wine
½ tsp. dried oregano
¼ tsp. freshly ground black pepper

½ tsp. dried thyme
½ tsp. of saffron
½ cup almond milk (unenriched)
¼ cup all-purpose flour
1 cup of water
2 ½ cups of white rice

1. Chop up the onion and mince the garlic cloves.
2. Mix the beef, stock, wine, onion, garlic, oregano, pepper, thyme and saffron in your slow cooker.
3. Cover and cook on High until the beef is tender, for about 4-5 hours.
4. Combine the almond milk, flour and water.
5. Whisk together until smooth.
6. Add the flour mixture to the slow cooker.
7. Cook for another 15 to 25 minutes until the stroganoff is thick.
8. Cook the rice using the package instructions, leaving out salt.
9. Drain off the excess water.
10. Serve the stroganoff over the rice.

Per Serving: Calories: 241
Protein: 15g
Carbohydrates: 29g
Fat: 5g
Cholesterol: 39g
Sodium: 182mg
Potassium: 206mg
Phosphorus: 151mg
Calcium: 59mg
Fiber: 1g

Beef Brisket with an Herby Sauce

SERVES 5 / PREP TIME: 15 MINUTES / COOK TIME: 8 HOURS

Succulent, chunky beef with a flavorful herb-infused sauce.

---

1 cup of onion
2 garlic cloves
10oz of flat cut beef brisket, whole
1 tbsp. of oregano
2 tsp. of Dijon mustard
1/2 tsp. of dried dill
1/2 tsp. of black pepper
½ cup of mushrooms, sliced

1/4 cup all-purpose white flour
1/4 cup of low-sodium beef stock
1 ½ cups of water

---

1. Chop the onion and mince the garlic.
2. Cut the brisket into 1/4" thick slices.
3. Place the steak, garlic, onions, seasonings and mushrooms in the slow cooker.
4. Stir it all well.
5. In a small bowl, gradually add the stock to the flour, stirring often.
6. Whisk it together until it's fully blended and free of lumps.
7. Add the broth mixture and the water to the pot and stir them in.
8. Cover with the lid and cook on High for 1 hour.
9. Reduce to Low and cook for 7 to 8 hours or until steak is tender.
10. Turn the slow cooker off, and remove lid.
11. Let the beef mixture stand for 10 minutes before serving.

Per Serving: Calories: 130
Protein: 15g
Carbohydrates: 5g
Fat: 5g
Cholesterol: 44mg
Sodium: 193mg
Potassium: 199mg
Phosphorus: 134mg
Calcium: 19mg
Fiber: 1g

Chunky Beef and Potato Slow Roast

SERVES 6 / PREP TIME: 15 MINUTES / COOK TIME: 5-6 HOURS

Chunky, warm and delicious, especially with a little horseradish kick on the side.

---

1 1/2 cups of peeled potatoes, chunked
1/2 cup of onion
1 garlic cloves, chopped
10oz flat cut beef brisket, fat trimmed
1 of cup water
1/2 tsp. of chili powder
1/2 tbsp. of dried rosemary

For the sauce::
1/2 tbsp. of freshly grated horseradish
1/4 cup of almond milk (unenriched)
1/2 tbsp. lemon juice (freshly squeezed)
1/2 garlic clove, minced
A pinch of cayenne pepper

---

1. Double boil the potatoes to reduce their potassium content.
2. (Hint: Bring your potato to the boil, then drain and refill with water to boil again.)
3. Chop the onion and the garlic.
4. Place the beef brisket in slow cooker.
5. Combine water, chopped garlic, chili powder and rosemary
6. Pour the mixture over the brisket.
7. Cover and cook on High for 4-5 hours until the meat is very tender.
8. Drain the potatoes and add them to the slow cooker.
9. Turn heat to High and cook covered until the potatoes are tender.
10. Prepare the horseradish sauce by whisking together horseradish, milk, lemon juice, minced garlic and cayenne pepper.
11. Cover and refrigerate.
12. Serve your casserole with a dash of horseradish sauce on the side.

Per Serving: Calories: 149
Protein: 15g
Carbohydrates: 11g
Fat: 5g
Cholesterol: 44mg
Sodium: 293mg
Potassium: 304
Phosphorus: 191mg
Calcium: 38mg
Fiber: 1g

Chinese-style Beef Stew

SERVES 6 / PREP TIME: 15 MINUTES / COOK TIME: 6-8 HOURS

A warm dish with vibrant flavors and a melt-in-the-mouth texture.

---

2 medium carrots
2 green onions
2 celery stalks
1 medium green bell pepper, sliced
1 garlic clove
8 oz. of canned bean sprouts
8 oz. of canned water chestnuts
2 tbsp. of coconut oil
12oz lean casserole beef, cut into cubes
½ cup low-sodium beef stock

1 tbsp. brown sugar
1/4 cup white wine vinegar
1 red chili, finely diced
1 ½ cups of water
3 cups cooked white rice

---

1. Slice the carrots, green onions, celery and green pepper.
2. Crush the garlic. (Hint: Use the flat edge of a knife to do this easily.)
3. Rinse and slice the bamboo shoots and water chestnuts.
4. Heat the coconut oil in a skillet and just brown the beef all over.
5. Transfer the beef to the slow cooker.
6. Add all the ingredients except the water.
7. Stir, then cover and cook on Low for 6 to 8 hours.
8. Turn the slow cooker up to High.
9. Add the cold water to the slow cooker.
10. Stir it in to make it smooth, and leave the cooker lid slightly open.
11. Cook for a further 15 minutes.
12. Serve your dish over a bed of rice.

Per Serving: Calories: 267
Protein: 14g
Carbohydrates: 31g
Fat: 9g
Cholesterol: 35mg
Sodium: 166mg
Potassium: 319mg
Phosphorus: 148mg
Calcium: 41mg
Fiber: 3g

Beef One-Pot Slow Roast

SERVES 8 / PREP TIME: 15 MINUTES / COOK TIME: 4-5 HOURS

A hot, hearty one-pot roast for large gatherings or cold evenings.

---

1 tbsp. plain flour
1 pound of boneless beef chuck or rump roast
1 tbsp. of olive oil
¼ cup leek, sliced
2 garlic cloves, minced
½ cup rutabaga, peeled and cubed
½ tsp. of dried thyme
1/2 tsp. of dried parsley
1 ½ cups water
¼ cup of carrots, sliced

---

1. First, dust the beef in flour.
2. In a hot oiled skillet, brown the meat on all sides.
3. Add the onions, then cover and cook on Low for 15 minutes.
4. Add the garlic, rutabaga, herb seasoning and 2 cups of water.
5. Add to the slow cooker and simmer on a medium heat for 3 ½ to 4 hours, until the meat is tender.
6. Finally, add in the carrots and cook for an additional 30 minutes.

Per Serving: Calories: 100
Protein: 12g
Carbohydrates: 2.5g
Fat: 4g
Cholesterol: 35.5mg
Sodium: 25.5mg
Potassium: 149mg
Phosphorus: 82.5mg
Calcium: 19mg
Fiber: 0.5g

Sticky Pork in Sweet and Sour Sauce

SERVES 4 / PREP TIME: 10 MINUTES / COOK TIME: 4 HOURS

A delicious blend of sweetness and acidity, with tender pork and light noodles.

8oz of lean pork roast, diced
1 cup of canned pineapple, juice drained
2 red bell peppers, diced
1 tsp. of soy sauce
1 tbsp. of tomato ketchup

1 tsp. of sage, dried
1 tbsp. red wine vinegar
2 cups of water
2 pak choy plants, washed and leaves pulled apart
2 cups of rice noodles
1 onion, chopped

1. Add all ingredients to a slow cooker, excluding the pak choy.
2. Leave to cook on High for 4-5 hours or on Low overnight.
3. 20 minutes before serving, add the rice noodles to a pan of boiling water and cook for 20 minutes or following package directions.
4. Add the pak choy leaves 10 minutes before serving.
5. Allow them to steam gently in the slow cooker.
6. In a deep dish, lay the noodles first, then spoon the pork and sauce on top.
7. Finally, add the steamed pak choy to finish.

Per Serving: Calories: 85
Protein: 9g
Carbohydrates: 9g
Fat: 1g
Cholesterol: 18mg
Sodium: 106mg
Potassium: 373mg
Phosphorus: 89mg
Calcium: 68mg
Fiber: 2g

Savory Pork and Bramley Apple Stew

SERVES 6 / PREP TIME: 10 MINUTES / COOK TIME: 8-10 HOURS

Soft, savory pork with the warm flavor of apple. A match made in heaven.

12oz of pork loin, whole
1 cup of Bramley apples, peeled and
cubed
A pinch of black pepper
1 tsp. of cloves
2 tbsp. of dried sage
4 cups of water

---

1. Rub the pork loin with the herbs and spices and place in the slow cooker.
2. Add the apple cubes and the water.
3. Add in the seasonings.
4. Cover and cook on Low for 8 to 10 hours.
5. Transfer the pork loin to a chopping board.
6. Leave it to rest for 5-10 minutes.
7. Carve the cooked loin into thick slices.
8. Serve the pork slices with the apple and the juices from the pot

Per Serving: Calories: 115
Protein: 15g
Carbohydrates: 5g
Fat: 4g
Cholesterol: 43mg
Sodium: 31mg
Potassium: 237mg
Phosphorus: 129mg
Calcium: 46mg
Fiber: 1g

Honey Mustard Marinated Pork Loin

SERVES 6 / PREP TIME: 10 MINUTES / COOK TIME: 4-5 HOURS

Sweet and tangy with tender vegetables and meltingly soft pork.

12oz of pork loin, boneless, fat-trimmed
and cubed
1 tbsp. of Dijon mustard
2 tbsp. of honey
2 tbsp. of coconut oil
1 medium white onion, roughly chopped
1 zucchini, roughly chopped
4 cups of water
1 tsp. of chili flakes
1 tsp. of dried sage
1 tsp. of ground nutmeg

---

1. Whisk together the honey, mustard and coconut oil.
2. Marinate the pork loin for at least 8 hours in the refrigerator.
3. Add the pork and remaining marinade to the slow cooker along with the vegetables.
4. Next, pour in the water and ensure the pork is well covered.
5. Sprinkle in the herbs and spices.
6. Cook on High for 4-5 hours.
7. Remove and serve steaming hot with white rice or rice noodles.

Per Serving: Calories: 134
Protein: 10g
Carbohydrates: 8g
Fat: 7g
Cholesterol: 29mg
Sodium: 60mg
Potassium: 235mg
Phosphorus: 100mg
Calcium: 29mg
Fiber: 1g

Cauliflower and Lamb Tagine

SERVES 5 / PREP TIME: 20 MINUTES / COOK TIME: 4-5 HOURS

The spices create a deep, authentic Moroccan flavor to the lamb with cauliflower to add a little crunch.

1 tbsp. of all-purpose flour
8oz of lean lamb, diced
1 tbsp. of olive oil
1 tbsp. of sweet paprika
1 tsp. cumin
1 tsp. of turmeric
1 red onion, diced
2 cups of cauliflower flowerets
4 cups water
4 white pita breads

1. In a shallow bowl with the flour, place the diced lamb.
2. Shake the bowl to dust the lamb.
3. Remove the lamb from the bowl.
4. Combine the spices in a measuring cup and evenly coat the floured lamb with the spices.
5. Heat the oil in a pan and then add the lamb cubes.
6. Brown on each side (5-10 minutes).
7. Transfer all the ingredients (minus the cauliflower) to the slow cooker.
8. Cook everything on High for 4-5 hours.
9. In the last 20 minutes, add the cauliflower florets and stir.
10. Lightly toast the pita breads when ready to serve.
11. Serve the tagine in a bowl with pita bread on the side for dipping.

Per Serving: Calories: 185
Protein: 14g
Carbohydrates: 17g
Fat: 7g
Cholesterol: 32mg
Sodium: 273mg
Potassium: 290mg
Phosphorus: 127mg
Calcium: 63mg
Fiber: 3g

Roasted Lamb with Mint and Garlic

SERVES 6 / PREP TIME: 15 MINUTES / COOK TIME: 5-6 HOURS

Lamb is at its best when rubbed with mint. Serve in thick slices for a succulent, tender roast.

10 oz. of lean lamb loin, boneless
3 garlic cloves, whole
1 tbsp. of olive oil
2 tbsp. of fresh mint, finely chopped
1 sheet of baking paper
2 cups zucchini, roughly chopped

2 cups carrots, peeled and roughly chopped
1 cup of water

1. Prepare the lamb by using a knife to make shallow carvings across the flesh.
2. Poke each garlic clove into the slices.
3. Mix the olive oil and mint to create a paste.
4. Rub this into the lamb.
5. Place the lamb in the slow cooker and cover baking paper.
6. Cook on high for 5-6 hours or until lamb is very soft.
7. In the last hour, add the carrots, zucchini and water.
8. Cook the vegetables until they're tender.
9. Serve hot with a drizzle of the lamb's lovely juices.

Per Serving: Calories: 153
Protein: 15g
Carbohydrates: 7g
Fat: 7g
Cholesterol: 44mg
Sodium: 223mg
Potassium: 420mg
Phosphorus: 147mg
Calcium: 44mg
Fiber: 2g

Roasted Lamb with Mint and Garlic

SERVES 6 / PREP TIME: 20 MINUTES / COOK TIME: 3 HOURS

Don't be put off by the long list of spices; they're worth it for the rich mellow flavor

---

2 red chilis, finely diced
1 tsp. cumin seeds
½ tbsp. fresh ginger, peeled and grated
3 cloves garlic, crushed
2 tbsp. of olive oil
1 cup white onions, sliced thinly

9oz lean lamb loin, washed, pat dry and cut into cubes
1 ½ cups almond milk (unenriched)
1/2 tsp. turmeric
1 tsp. cardamom pods, crushed slightly
1 ½ cups white rice
¼ cup chopped fresh cilantro

---

1. Grind the red chilies, cumin seeds, ginger and garlic together into a smooth paste using a blender or pestle and mortar.
2. Heat the oil in a pan over a medium heat and sauté the onions until golden.
3. Add the spice paste to the pan and stir until the oil separates from the mixture.
4. Now, add the lamb pieces and brown for 5 minutes whilst stirring.
5. Add the almond milk and turmeric and mix well.
6. Transfer to the slow cooker and add the star anise and cardamom pods.
7. Cook on a low heat for 2 hours until the lamb is very tender.
8. 20 minutes before serving, pour 6 cups of cold water to a pan.
9. Add the rice to the water and bring to a boil.
10. Turn down the heat and simmer for another 15 minutes.
11. Drain and return to pan with the lid on for 5 minutes to steam.
12. Serve with freshly steamed rice and garnish with fresh cilantro.

Per Serving: Calories: 204
Protein: 15g
Carbohydrates: 19g
Fat: 7g
Cholesterol: 40mg
Sodium: 214mg
Potassium: 379mg
Phosphorus: 133mg
Calcium: 139mg
Fiber: 1g

Roast Pork and Tangy Cabbage Slaw

SERVES 4 / PREP TIME: 20 MINUTES / COOK TIME: 8 HOURS

Lightly spiced pork, aromatic cloves and a crunchy, zesty slaw. Great for barbecues.

1 tsp. of nutmeg
1 tsp. of allspice
1 tbsp. of dried sage
1 tbsp. of olive oil
8oz of lean pork loin
1 tsp. of cloves
2 white of onions, chopped
2 cups of water
2 carrots, peeled and grated

1 cup of white cabbage, washed and grated or spiralized
1 lime, juiced

1. Mix nutmeg, allspice and sage with olive oil to form a marinade.
2. Coat the pork and marinate for as long as you can.
3. When ready to cook, evenly press the cloves into the pork.
4. Add the pork loin with the onions and water to the slow cooker.
5. Cook on Medium for 8 hours until the pork is very soft.
6. Meanwhile, prepare your slaw.
7. Mix the carrot and cabbage, and squeeze over the lime juice.
8. Cover and place in the fridge until you're ready to serve.
9. Remove the loin and slice generously.
10. Serve with the slaw, a helping of onions and a drizzle of the juices.
11. Don't forget to pick out the cloves before serving!

Per Serving: Calories: 129
Protein: 10g
Carbohydrates: 13g
Fat: 5g
Cholesterol: 23mg
Sodium: 25mg
Potassium: 343mg
Phosphorus: 109mg
Calcium: 60mg
Fiber: 3g

Chili Pork and Rice Noodles

SERVES 5 / PREP TIME:5 MINUTES / COOK TIME: 1.5 HOURS

Light rice noodles and chili infused pork, this is a dish to add to your go-to recipe list.

---

1 tbsp. olive oil
2 white onions, diced
2 garlic cloves, minced
1 red chili, finely diced
8oz lean ground pork
2 cups water
1 tsp. oregano
1 tsp. dried basil
1 tbsp. balsamic vinegar

2 cups of rice noodles
A pinch of black pepper

---

1. Heat the oil in a skillet over a medium-high heat.
2. Add the onions and sauté them for 5 minutes until soft.
3. Add in the garlic and chili and sauté for a further 5 minutes.
4. Add the ground pork and cook until its' browned (5-10 minutes).
5. Pour the pork mixture into the slow cooker
6. Add the water, herbs and vinegar.
7. The pork should be just covered but not swimming.
8. Cook on the High for 1 hour.
9. The sauce should be nice and thick at this point.
10. While waiting, prepare your pasta by following the package directions.
11. Serve the cooked spaghetti with a serving of pork chili and a pinch of sprinkled black pepper on top.

Per Serving: Calories: 286
Protein: 14g
Carbohydrates: 29g
Fat: 12g
Cholesterol: 42mg
Sodium: 200mg
Potassium: 351mg
Phosphorus: 153mg
Calcium: 54mg
Fiber: 2g

Roast Beef and Chunky Vegetable Stew

SERVES 8/ PREP TIME: 15 MINUTES / COOK TIME: 8-10 HOURS

Deliciously hearty and beautifully filling.

---

1 cup of rutabaga, peeled and cut into cubes
1 cup of potato, peeled and cut into cubes
1 cup of carrots, cut into 2-inch pieces
1 red onion, cut into wedges
3 cloves garlic, finely chopped

1 tbsp. of olive oil
16oz of flat cut beef brisket
1 tsp. of freshly ground pepper
1 cup of low sodium chicken stock
½ cup of water
3 tbsp. of chopped fresh parsley

---

1. Spray your slow cooker dish with a little cooking spray.
2. In the slow cooker, stir together the rutabaga, potato, carrots, onion and garlic.
3. In a large skillet, heat the oil over medium-high heat.
4. Sprinkle the beef with ground pepper and lay it in the skillet.
5. Cook until browned evenly on all sides.
6. Place the vegetables in the slow cooker.
7. Lay the beef on top.
8. Pour the stock and water over the beef.
9. Cover and cook on Low for 8 to 10 hours or until the beef is very tender.
10. Serve the beef along with the vegetables and the juices.
11. Garnish the top with a sprinkle of fresh parsley.

Per Serving: Calories: 151
Protein: 13g
Carbohydrates: 11g
Fat: 6g
Cholesterol: 36mg
Sodium: 101mg
Potassium: 373mg
Phosphorus: 140mg
Calcium: 33mg
Fiber: 2g

Ginger and Lemon Lamb with Noodles

SERVES 5 / PREP TIME: 10 MINUTES / COOK TIME: 2.5 HOURS

Delicate lamb with zesty flavors of lemon and ginger.

8oz lean lamb loin
1 tbsp. of coconut oil
1 tbsp. of fresh root ginger, finely sliced
4 garlic cloves
1 tbsp. of soft light brown sugar
Rind of 1 lemon
1 bunch of scallions

1 cup of pak choy, leaves separated
4 cups of rice noodles

---

1. Place the lamb in an oiled slow cooker dish.
2. Cook on High for 15 minutes to start.
3. Meanwhile, peel and slice the ginger and the garlic.
4. Add to the slow cooker with the sugar and lemon.
5. Cover the ingredients with water.
6. Cook on High for a further 15 minutes.
7. Reduce to Medium and cover the lamb with baking paper.
8. Cook for a further 2 hours or until the lamb is very tender.
9. Carve the lamb into nice thick slices.
10. Place the lamb on a warmed serving platter.
11. Cover it up and keep it warm in a low oven.
12. Roughly chop the scallions and thickly slice the pak choy.
13. Cook the noodles according to package directions.
14. Stir in the scallions and pak choy leaves.
15. Return to the boil and bubble, they only need a minute or so.
16. Serve the noodles immediately with the slices of lamb on top and the juices drizzled over.

Per Serving: Calories: 264
Protein: 15g
Carbohydrates: 33g
Fat: 7g
Cholesterol: 43mg
Sodium: 222mg
Potassium: 343mg
Phosphorus: 144mg
Calcium: 60mg
Fiber: 2g

POULTRY

Chicken and Squash Slow Roast

SERVES 8 / PREP TIME: 20 MINUTES / COOK TIME: 8-10 HOURS

This is a great winter warming dish for family gatherings or just some good comfort food.

3oz of all-purpose flour
1 tbsp. of coconut oil
10oz of boneless, skinless chicken breast, chopped
1 red onion, chopped
3 garlic cloves, finely chopped
1 tsp. of chili powder
1 spaghetti squash, cut into half (horizontally)
1 cup of low sodium chicken stock
1 cup of water

5 sprigs of fresh thyme (or 1 tbsp. dried)
3 bay leaves
A pinch of black pepper
2 tbsp. of chopped fresh parsley (optional)

1. Sprinkle the flour onto a plate.
2. Heat half of the oil in a skillet.
3. Dust the chicken pieces in the flour.
4. Cook the chicken for 4-5 minutes, or until browned all over. (Hint: You may need to brown the chicken a little at a time.)
5. Tip the chicken into the slow cooker.
6. Heat the remaining oil in a skillet and fry the onion until clear
7. Add in the garlic and cook for another 2-3 minutes.
8. Tip the onion mixture into the slow cooker too.
9. Add the chicken stock, thyme, chili powder and bay leaves to the slow cooker.
10. Stir everything together, pressing down so that everything is covered in liquid.
11. Press each half of the spaghetti squash into the mixture (skin side up).
12. Cook for 8-10 hours on Low.
13. Stir in the black pepper and parsley before serving.

Per Serving: Calories: 145
Protein: 15g
Carbohydrates: 13g
Fat: 4g
Cholesterol: 41mg
Sodium: 237mg
Potassium: 266mg
Phosphorus: 128mg
Calcium: 21mg
Fiber: 1g

Smoky Turkey Chili

SERVES 8 / PREP TIME: 5 MINUTES / COOK TIME: 45 MINUTES

Succulent, smoky and mildly spiced. A perfect blend to sizzle your taste buds.

12oz lean ground turkey
1/2 red onion, chopped
2 cloves garlic, crushed and chopped
½ tsp. of smoked paprika
½ tsp. of chili powder
½ tsp. of dried thyme

¼ cup reduced-sodium beef stock
½ cup of water
1 ½ cups baby spinach leaves, washed
3 wheat tortillas

---

1. Brown the ground beef in a dry skillet over a medium-high heat.
2. Add in the red onion and garlic.
3. Sauté the onion until it goes clear.
4. Transfer the contents of the skillet to the slow cooker.
5. Add the remaining ingredients and simmer on Low for 30–45 minutes.
6. Stir through the spinach for the last few minutes to wilt.
7. Slice tortillas and gently toast under the broiler until slightly crispy.
8. Serve on top of the turkey chili.

Per Serving: Calories: 93.5
Protein: 8g
Carbohydrates: 3g
Fat: 5.5g
Cholesterol: 30.5mg
Sodium: 84.5mg
Potassium: 142.5mg
Phosphorus: 92.5mg
Calcium: 29mg
Fiber: 0.5g

Aromatic Spiced Chicken Curry

SERVES 4 / PREP TIME: 5 MINUTES / COOK TIME: 4-5 HOURS

Tender chicken with rich warming spices, incredibly easy and an impressive meal.

1 tbsp. of olive oil
1 onion, diced
1 tsp. of mild curry powder
1 carrot, peeled and diced
1 tsp. of turmeric
1 tsp. of allspice
1 tsp. of cumin

8oz of skinless chicken breast, diced
2 cups of water
A pinch of black pepper
2 cups of cooked white rice
2 tbsp. of fresh cilantro

1. Heat the oil in a large wok or skillet over a medium-high heat.
2. Add the onions and sauté for five minutes to soften (but not brown) them.
3. Now add the turmeric and stir briefly.
4. Next, add the allspice and stir.
5. Add the cumin and stir.
6. Transfer the onion mixture into the slow cooker.
7. Cook the chicken in the skillet until all sides are white.
8. Transfer to a slow cooker with the rest of the ingredients (minus the rice).
9. Cook for 4-5 hours on High or overnight on Low.
10. Serve your curry with white rice and a sprinkle of fresh cilantro.

Per Serving: Calories: 213
Protein: 15g
Carbohydrates: 25g
Fat: 5g
Cholesterol: 35mg
Sodium: 44mg
Potassium: 210mg
Phosphorus: 140mg
Calcium: 43mg
Fiber: 1g

Turmeric Curried Chicken

SERVES 6 / PREP TIME: 15 MINUTES / COOK TIME: 5 HOURS

Soft, juicy chicken with a delicious curry sauce with a little bit of a kick.

8oz skinless, boneless chicken breast
1 red bell pepper, chopped
1 yellow bell pepper, chopped
1 small white onion, sliced
1 fresh red chili pepper, de-seeded and finely chopped
2 cloves of garlic, minced
1 cup of low-sodium chicken stock
3 tbsp. of curry powder

1/4 tsp. of turmeric
1/2 cup almond milk (unenriched)
1 tsp. of cornstarch
2 cups white rice, cooked
2 tbsp. of fresh cilantro, chopped

---

1. Combine the chicken, peppers, onion, chili, garlic, stock, curry powder and turmeric in the slow cooker.
2. Cover and cook on Low for 8- 9 hours or on High for about 4½ hours.
3. In a small bowl, mix the almond milk and cornstarch until smooth.
4. Stir into chicken mixture.
5. If you're cooking on Low, turn up the heat to High now.
6. Cover and cook for 15 to 20 minutes more.
7. The sauce should be slightly thick by now.
8. Serve on white rice and sprinkle the with cilantro to finish.

Per Serving: Calories: 182
Protein: 15g
Carbohydrates: 25g
Fat: 3g
Cholesterol: 36mg
Sodium: 213mg
Potassium: 390mg
Phosphorus: 155mg
Calcium: 76mg
Fiber: 2g

Fennel and Ginger Chicken

SERVES 6 /   PREP TIME: 1 MINUTES /   COOK TIME: 2-3 HOURS

Tastes just as good without the meat!

12oz of skinless boneless chicken breast, diced
1/4 tsp. ground black pepper
1 bulb fennel, cored and cut into thin wedges
1 red bell pepper, de-seeded and diced
1 medium red onion, diced
3 cloves of garlic, minced
1 tsp. fresh or dried rosemary
1 tsp. of fresh or dried ginger (finely sliced if fresh)

½ cup reduced-sodium chicken stock
½ cup of water
1 tbsp. of dried oregano

---

1. Sprinkle the chicken pieces with ground pepper.
2. Place the chicken into the slow cooker.
3. Top with fennel, bell pepper, onion, garlic, rosemary and ginger.
4. Add the stock and water.
5. Cover and cook on Low for 5 to 6 hours or on High for 2½ to 3 hours.
6. Sprinkle each serving with oregano to finish.

Per Serving: Calories: 95
Protein: 15g
Carbohydrates: 4g
Fat: 2g
Cholesterol: 45mg
Sodium: 270mg
Potassium: 348mg
Phosphorus: 130mg
Calcium: 35mg
Fiber: 1g

Spanish-style Chicken

SERVES 5 / PREP TIME: 5 MINUTES / COOK TIME: 3 ½ -4 HOURS

This blend of spices brings a smoky and intense flavor to the table.

10oz skinless, boneless chicken thighs, cut into cubes
2 large red onions, roughly chopped
1 garlic clove, minced
½ tsp. of dried oregano
¼ tsp. of ground black pepper
1 cup of reduced-sodium chicken stock

1 cup of water
1 medium red bell pepper, roughly chopped
1 tsp. of paprika
1 tsp. of cumin
2 cups of cooked white rice

1. In the slow cooker, combine the chicken, onion, garlic, oregano and black pepper.
2. Add in the stock and water.
3. Cover and cook on Low for 7 to 8 hours or on High for 3 ½ to 4 hours.
4. If using Low, turn the heat up to High at this point.
5. Stir in the red pepper, paprika and cumin.
6. Cover and cook for another 30 minutes.
7. Serve steaming hot with fluffy white rice.

Per Serving: Calories: 188
Protein: 11g
Carbohydrates: 29g
Fat: 3g
Cholesterol: 39mg
Sodium: 46mg
Potassium: 343mg
Phosphorus: 143mg
Calcium: 44mg
Fiber: 2g

Tender Spice-Rubbed Turkey Thighs

SERVES 4 / PREP TIME: 5 MINUTES / COOK TIME: 7-8 HOURS

Fragrant spices, juicy turkey and a tangy salsa on the side.

---

1 tsp. of cumin
1 tsp. of cinnamon
1 tsp. of chili powder
1 tsp. of dried oregano
1 garlic clove, minced
8oz of turkey thighs, skinless and boneless

A pinch of black pepper
1 red onion, soaked in warm water
1 lime, juiced
2 tbsp. of fresh cilantro, chopped

Mix the dry spices, herbs and minced garlic in a bowl to form a rub.

Rub the turkey thighs with the spice mix.

Place in the bottom of the slow cooker in a single layer.

Cook for 7-8 hours on a low setting.

Meanwhile, prepare your salsa. (Hint: Do this the night before and refrigerate for a better flavor.)

Finely dice the red onion and mix it with the fresh lime juice.

Remove the turkey thighs from the slow cooker.

Place them onto a chopping board.

Cut the thighs into slices.

Sprinkle the cilantro into the salsa before serving.

Serve on a plate with a helping of salsa.

Per Serving: Calories: 113
Protein: 15g
Carbohydrates: 8g
Fat: 3g
Cholesterol: 60mg
Sodium: 260mg
Potassium: 245mg
Phosphorus: 131mg
Calcium: 41mg
Fiber: 2g

Turkey and Lemon Rice Stew

SERVES 5 / PREP TIME: 15 MINUTES / COOK TIME: 6-7 HOURS

Tender turkey with a twist of lemon, and a salad to bring it all together with crunch.

---

1 tbsp. of olive oil
8oz of turkey breast tenderloins, skinless and boneless, diced
½ cup chopped celery
1/3 cup of chopped carrot
¼ cup of chopped red onion
1 cup of low sodium chicken stock
1 cup of water

1 tsp. of dried oregano
A pinch of black pepper
1.5 cups of white rice, rinsed and drained
1 lemon, juiced
1 cucumber, washed and sliced
1 cup of romaine lettuce or similar, washed
2 tbsp. of extra virgin olive oil

---

1. Heat the oil in a skillet over a medium heat.
2. Add in the turkey breast.
3. Cook for 3-5 minutes, stirring often until the turkey is brown.
4. Stir in the celery, carrot and onion.
5. Cook for 2 minutes, stirring occasionally.
6. Drain off the excess juices.
7. In the slow cooker, mix the turkey mixture and remaining ingredients except lemon, extra virgin olive oil, cucumber and lettuce.
8. Cover with the lid and cook on High for 30 minutes.
9. Reduce the heat to a Low.
10. Cook for 6-7 hours, or until the rice is tender and the liquid is absorbed.
11. Stir in the juice of half a lemon.
12. Slice the cucumber and lettuce for the side salad.
13. Whisk the remaining lemon juice and olive oil together.
14. Dress the salad with the lemon and oil dressing.
15. Serve on the side of your turkey.

Per Serving: Calories: 207
Protein: 12g
Carbohydrates: 20g
Fat: 9g
Cholesterol: 26mg
Sodium: 53mg
Potassium: 339mg
Phosphorus: 131mg
Calcium: 43mg
Fiber: 2g

Moroccan-Style Apricot Turkey Stew

SERVES 8 / PREP TIME: 5 MINUTES / COOK TIME: 3 ½ -4 HOURS

Rich spices, soft turkey and the sweetness of apricot come together for a delicious family meal.

4 carrots, peeled and sliced
2 large red onions, thinly sliced
12oz of turkey breast, skinless and boneless, diced
½ cup of canned apricots, drained and coarsely chopped
1 cup of low sodium chicken stock
2 tbsp. of all-purpose flour
2 tbsp. of lemon juice, freshly squeezed

2 cloves of garlic, minced
1 ½ tsp. of ground cumin
1 ½ tsp. of ground ginger
1 tsp. of ground nutmeg
¾ tsp. of ground black pepper
3 cups of cooked white rice
3 tbsp. of fresh cilantro, finely chopped

1. Add the carrots and onions into the slow cooker.
2. Add the diced turkey to cooker too, and top with the apricots.
3. In bowl, whisk the stock, flour, lemon juice, garlic, cumin, ginger, nutmeg and the ground black pepper.
4. Add the mixture to the cooker.
5. Cover and cook on Low for 6 ½ to 7 hours or on High for 3 ½ to 4 hours.
6. Serve the rice in bowls with the turkey and the sauce on top.
7. Garnish with cilantro to finish.

Per Serving: Calories: 189
Protein: 13g
Carbohydrates: 33g
Fat: 1g
Cholesterol: 24mg
Sodium: 45mg
Potassium: 371mg
Phosphorus: 144mg
Calcium: 45mg
Fiber: 3g

One-Pot Chinese-style Chicken

SERVES 4 / PREP TIME: 15 MINUTES / COOK TIME: 6-8 HOURS

A quick and delicious version of a classic Chinese dish.

2 carrots, peeled and sliced
2 green onions, finely chopped
4 celery stalks, sliced
2 garlic cloves, minced
2 tbsp. of sesame oil
8oz of boneless, skinless chicken breast, diced
1 cup of low-sodium chicken stock
1 tsp. of low-sodium soy sauce
1 tbsp. of Chinese five-spice
1 tsp. of fresh ginger, minced

⅓ cup of water
2 cups of snow peas
3 cups of cooked white rice
1 lime, juiced

1. Slice the carrots, green onions and celery.
2. Crush the garlic.
3. Heat the oil in a skillet and add the diced chicken.
4. Cook the chicken until it's nicely browned all over.
5. Transfer the chicken from the skillet to the slow cooker.
6. Add all the other ingredients (except the lime juice and snow peas).
7. Stir, then cover up and cook on a Low for 6 to 8 hours.
8. In the last 10 minutes, add the snow peas to the slow cooker.
9. Put on the lid slightly ajar to allow the peas to steam.
10. Serve the chicken and vegetables over rice with a squeeze of fresh lime.

Per Serving: Calories: 127
Protein: 11g
Carbohydrates: 8g
Fat: 6g
Cholesterol: 23mg
Sodium: 93mg
Potassium: 350mg
Phosphorus: 111mg
Calcium: 57mg
Fiber: 3g

Barbecue Pulled Chicken Rolls

SERVES 8 / PREP TIME: 5 MINUTES / COOK TIME: 6 HOURS

Sweet, smoky and melt-in-the-mouth with a tingle of spice.

16oz skinless, skinless boneless chicken breast fillets, whole
2 tbsp. of mustard
2 tsp. of lemon juice
1 garlic clove, finely grated
1/4 cup of brown sugar
1/2 tsp. of chili powder

1 tbsp. of tomato ketchup
4 white hamburger rolls, sliced in half
3 cups of arugula, washed

---

1. Place the chicken breasts into the bottom of the slow cooker.
2. In a bowl, stir together the mustard, lemon juice, garlic, brown sugar, chili powder and tomato ketchup.
3. Mix it together well.
4. Pour in the sauce, set the cooker to Low and cook for 6 hours.
5. Shred the chicken with two forks and cook for 30 more minutes.
6. Serve the chicken and sauce spooned onto each half of the hamburger bun with the arugula on top.

Per Serving: Calories: 141
Protein: 15g
Carbohydrates: 14g
Fat: 2g
Cholesterol: 35mg
Sodium: 160mg
Potassium: 177mg
Phosphorus: 121mg
Calcium: 56mg
Fiber: 1g

Stuffed Roast Chicken

SERVES 10 / PREP TIME: 20 MINUTES / COOK TIME: 4 HOURS 15 MINS

A classic roast. Juicy, indulgent and stuffed to perfection.

---

3 pounds of whole chicken, giblets removed
1 tsp. of olive oil
1 tsp. of ground black pepper
1 carrot, peeled and chopped
2 garlic cloves, whole
½ medium red onion, quartered
1 medium celery stalk, roughly chopped

¼ cup of white breadcrumbs
1 cup of broccoli florets

---

1. Trim any excess fat off the chicken.
2. In a food processor, mix everything but the chicken and broccoli.
3. This is for your stuffing.
4. Stuff the chicken cavity.
5. Place the whole chicken into the slow cooker.
6. Cook on High for 4 hours, until the thigh and leg easily pull away and the meat easily comes off the bones.
7. Remove the skin and discard.
8. Remove the meat from the bones and place to one side.
9. Weigh the meat before serving – you should serve only 2oz of chicken per person.
10. Prepare the broccoli by steaming for 10-15 minutes.
11. Serve the roasted chicken with the steamed broccoli.
12. (Hint: Allow the rest of the meat to cool before covering and placing in fridge for 2-3 days or freezer for 2-3 weeks.)
13. You can also use the stock from the slow cooker – simply sieve out any chunks and allow to cool. Repeat above.

Per Serving: Calories: 87   Fiber: 1g
Protein: 13.5g
Carbohydrates: 4g
Fat: 2g
Cholesterol: 40.5mg
Sodium: 224mg
Potassium: 248mg
Phosphorus: 115.5mg
Calcium: 25mg

VEGETARIAN AND VEGAN

Winter Spiced Squash Stew

SERVES 6 / PREP TIME: 15 MINUTES / COOK TIME: 6-7 HOURS

A Winter favorite with soft, sweet squash and warm flavors.

---

1 spaghetti squash
2 medium zucchini
1/2 cup of yellow bell pepper
1 cup of unsweetened canned pineapple, diced
½ cup of water
1 tsp. of allspice
2 ½ tbsp. of brown sugar substitute
1 tbsp. of unsalted butter

---

1. Cut the squashes down the middle (horizontally).
2. Dice the bell pepper into small pieces.
3. Placed the squash halves into the slow cooker (skin side up).
4. In a small bowl, mix the pepper, pineapple, ½ cup of water, allspice, brown sugar and melted butter.
5. Pour the mix into the slow cooker around the base of the squash.
6. Cover the squash and cook on a Low for 6-7 hours or until squash is tender.
7. Stir the pot gently to mix the ingredients well before serving.

Per Serving: Calories: 63
Protein: 1g
Carbohydrates: 10g
Fat: 3g
Cholesterol: 5mg
Sodium: 18mg
Potassium: 309mg
Phosphorus: 37mg
Calcium: 38mg
Fiber: 2g

Vegetable Stew with Mediterranean Spices

SERVES 4 / PREP TIME: 10 MINUTES / COOK TIME: 1-2 HOURS

Soft and sweet with a beautiful blend of spices.

1 zucchini, sliced
2 red bell peppers, sliced
2 eggplants, diced
2 medium white onions, diced
3 cups of water
1 cup of low sodium vegetable stock (optional)
1 tsp. of dried thyme
1 tsp. of nutmeg
1 tsp. of paprika
1 tbsp. of cider vinegar
1 tbsp. of ground black pepper
1 tbsp. all-purpose flour
2 garlic cloves, peeled and halved
2 cups white rice

2 tbsp. fresh basil, chopped

1. Wash and roughly chop the vegetables into large pieces.
2. Bring the water to a boil in a saucepan.
3. Mix the flour with the boiled water until the lumps dissolve.
4. Now add all the ingredients into the slow cooker.
5. Cook on Low for 1-2 hours or until the vegetables are soft and the sauce is thickened.
6. Serve with fluffy white rice and a garnish of fresh basil.

Per Serving: Calories: 154
Protein: 4g
Carbohydrates: 34g
Fat: 1g
Cholesterol: 0mg
Sodium: 132mg
Potassium: 380mg
Phosphorus: 85mg
Calcium: 63mg
Fiber: 4

Chunky Root Vegetable Roast

SERVES 6 / PREP TIME: 10 MINUTES / COOK TIME: 3-4 HOURS

Best served steaming hot with helping of crusty white bread on the side.

---

1 rutabaga, peeled and cubed
2 large carrots, peeled and cubed
2 turnips, peeled and cubed
2 cups of water
1 tbsp. of all-purpose flour
1 garlic clove, minced

1 cup of low sodium vegetable stock
(optional)
2 tbsp. dried oregano
1 tbsp. black pepper
1 loaf of crusty white bread

---

1. Peel and chop the rutabaga, carrots and turnips into cubes.
2. Boil the water and stir in the flour until lumps have dissolved.
3. Add all of the remaining ingredients to the slow cooker.
4. Cook on a Low 3-4 hours or until vegetables are tender.
5. Serve in hearty bowls.
6. Toast the bread and serve it on the side of the casserole.
7. Dip and enjoy!

Per Serving: Calories: 144
Protein: 5g
Carbohydrates: 29g
Fat: 1g
Cholesterol: 0mg
Sodium: 265mg
Potassium: 388mg
Phosphorus: 92mg
Calcium: 169mg
Fiber: 4g

Soft Red Cabbage with Cranberry

SERVES 5 / PREP TIME: 15 MINUTES / COOK TIME: 1 HOUR

A mix of sweet and tart flavors. Try this as a side dish for Thanksgiving.

---

2 red cabbages
1 cup of canned cranberries, juices
drained
1 tsp. of balsamic vinegar
1 tsp. of allspice
1 tsp. of ground black pepper
1 tsp. of brown sugar substitute
2 cups of water

---

1. Wash and slice the red cabbage, making sure it's not too thin.
2. Throw all of the ingredients into the slow cooker.
3. Cook on Low for 1 hour or until the cabbage is soft.
4. Enjoy this as a main dish with rice or noodles or as a side dish.

Per Serving: Calories: 107
Protein: 2g
Carbohydrates: 27g
Fat: 0g
Cholesterol: 0mg
Sodium: 50mg
Potassium: 335mg
Phosphorus: 44mg
Calcium: 67mg
Fiber: 4g

Slow Cooked Cabbage with Cucumber and Dill Relish

SERVES 4 / PREP TIME: 5 MINUTES / COOK TIME: 1.5 HOURS

The tender slow cooked cabbage is complemented with a cool, crisp relish for something a little different.

---

1 white cabbage
1 tbsp. of olive oil
1 lemon, juice squeezed
A pinch of black pepper
1 cucumber, diced
1 tbsp. of fresh or dried dill

---

1. Slice the cabbage into strips.
2. Melt the butter in a skillet over a medium heat and add the juice from half of the lemon (save one half for serving).
3. Pour this into the slow cooker and add in the cabbage.
4. Cover with a little water, just to reach the top of the cabbage.
5. Cook on a Low with the lid on for 1 ½ hours.
6. Remove the lid and continue to cook if it's still a bit watery for 10 minutes.
7. Prepare your salad by dicing the cucumber and mixing in the dill.
8. Squeeze the leftover lemon juice into the salad.
9. Serve a helping of the cabbage with the cool cucumber relish.

Per Serving: Calories: 73
Protein: 2g
Carbohydrates: 10g
Fat: 4g
Cholesterol: 0mg
Sodium: 13mg
Potassium: 375mg
Phosphorus: 61mg
Calcium: 80mg
Fiber: 3g

SOUPS, SIDES & STOCKS

Tarragon, Carrot and Lemon Soup

SERVES 4 / PREP TIME: 15 MINUTES / COOK TIME: 7-8 HOURS

A lovely hot, warming soup with a little added zest.

1 tbsp. of olive oil
1 tsp. of mustard seeds, ground
1 tsp. of fennel seeds, ground
1 tbsp. of oregano
1 tbsp. of ground ginger
6 medium carrots, peeled and chopped
1 red onion, diced
1 lemon, zest and juice

4 cups of water
1 tsp. of ground black pepper

1. Heat the oil in a skillet over a medium heat.
2. Once hot, add the mustard and fennel seeds.
3. Cook them for just a minute.
4. Add the ginger and cook for another minute.
5. Add the carrots, onions and lemon juice.
6. Cook them for at least 5 minutes or until the vegetables are soft.
7. Add all the cooked ingredients to the slow cooker.
8. Add in the water and the oregano, too.
9. Cook on Low for about 7-8 hours.
10. Serve with the black pepper sprinkled on top.

Per Serving : Calories: 99
Protein: 2g
Carbohydrates: 26g
Fat: 4g
Cholesterol: 0mg
Sodium: 68mg
Potassium: 378mg
Phosphorus: 58mg
Calcium: 87mg
Fiber: 5g

Coconut and Lemongrass Turkey Soup

SERVES 6 / PREP TIME: 15 MINUTES / COOK TIME: 4-6 HOURS

Full of bold, zesty flavors to add a twist to a wholesome turkey soup.

½ stick of lemongrass, sliced
1 tbsp. of cilantro
1 red chili, finely chopped
1 tbsp. of coconut oil
1 tbsp. of oregano
1 white onion, chopped
1 garlic clove, minced
1 tbsp. of ground ginger

12oz of skinless turkey breast, diced
½ cup of water
½ cup of low-sodium chicken stock
1 fresh lime, juiced
½ cup of pak choy leaves, shredded
1 cup of canned water chestnuts
2 green onions, chopped

---

1. Crush the lemongrass, cilantro, chili, coconut oil and oregano in a blender or pestle and mortar to form a paste.
2. Heat a large pan/wok with 1 tbsp. coconut oil on a high heat.
3. Sauté the onions, garlic and ginger until soft.
4. Add the turkey cubes and brown evenly on each side.
5. Add the water and stir. Now add the paste.
6. Slowly add the stock until a broth is formed.
7. Now add all of the ingredients from the wok to the slow cooker.
8. Squeeze in the lime juice.
9. Cook everything on Low for 4-6 hours.
10. Add the pak choy and water chestnuts 20 minutes before serving.
11. Serve steaming with the green onion sprinkled over the top.

Per Serving: Calories: 115
Protein: 13g
Carbohydrates: 10g
Fat: 3g
Cholesterol: 32mg
Sodium: 37mg
Potassium: 323mg
Phosphorus: 122mg
Calcium: 47mg
Fiber: 2g

Tender Pork and White Cabbage Soup

SERVES 6 / PREP TIME: 10 MINUTES / COOK TIME: 7-8 HOURS

A classic mix of soft, succulent pork and cabbage for a warming, hearty soup.

½ tbsp. of olive oil
½ red onion, chopped
1 garlic cloves, minced
6oz of lean pork loin
½ cup of low-sodium chicken stock
1 cup of water
½ tbsp. of allspice
½ cup of white cabbage, sliced
½ tsp. of black pepper

1. Trim the fat from the pork loin meat and slice into 1 inch thick slices.
2. Heat up the oil in a wok.
3. Add the onion and garlic and sauté for 5 minutes on a low heat.
4. Add the pork to the wok and cook for 7-8 minutes to brown.
5. Transfer the ingredients from the wok to the slow cooker.
6. Pour the stock and water into the slow cooker.
7. Add in the allspice to season.
8. Add the in sliced cabbage and stir the pot well.
9. Cook on Low for a further 7-8 hours until the pork is very soft.
10. Sprinkle with the black pepper to finish.

Per Serving: Calories: 84
Protein: 14g
Carbohydrates: 3g
Fat: 4g
Cholesterol: 22.5mg
Sodium: 117mg
Potassium: 187.5mg
Phosphorus: 85.5mg
Calcium: 21.5mg
Fiber: 0.5g

Rustic Low Sodium Stock with Vegetables

SERVES 10 / PREP TIME: 10 MINUTES / COOK TIME: 4-6 HOURS

A classic base for any sauce-based recipe.

---

2 onions, diced
3 carrots, peeled and chopped
3 celery stalks, chopped
1 garlic clove
1 bay leaf
1 tbsp. of rosemary
1 tbsp. of oregano

1 tbsp. of dried parsley
1 tsp. of whole black peppercorns
5 cups of water
1 tbsp. of olive oil

---

1. Peel and roughly chop the vegetables.
2. Soak them in warm water for 10 minutes.
3. Add the vegetables, garlic, herbs and peppercorns into the slow cooker.
4. Fill up the slow cooker with boiling water and add the oil.
5. Cook on High for roughly 4-6 hours.
6. Strain the stock using a sieve.
7. Use immediately or allow to it cool and refrigerate.
8. If refrigerated, use within 2-3 days or freeze for 3-4 weeks in a sealed container.

Per Serving: Calories: 41
Protein: 1g
Carbohydrates: 7g
Fat: 2g
Cholesterol: 0mg
Sodium: 22mg
Potassium: 153mg
Phosphorus: 24mg
Calcium: 29mg
Fiber: 2g

Rustic Low Sodium Stock with Chicken

SERVES 15 / PREP TIME: 5 MINUTES / COOK TIME: 40 MINUTES

Don't miss out on this chunky Asian-infused soup.

---

2 pounds of roasting chicken, (half a chicken)
1 1/2 carrots, soaked in warm water
1 medium onion
1 1/2 stalks of celery, soaked in warm water
2 garlic cloves, crushed
1 bay leaves
1/2 tbsp. dried rosemary
1/2 tbsp. of dried thyme
1/2 tbsp. of ground black pepper
1/2 tbsp. of dried parsley
6-7 cups of water
1/2 tbsp. of cider vinegar

---

1. Rinse off the chicken and place it in a large saucepan or soup pan.
2. (Hint: Remove the giblets but don't waste them; add them in to your stock bowl!)
3. Wash and chop your vegetables into large chunks, leaving the skins on.
4. Add the chunks into the pan, too.
5. Add the herbs, spices and black pepper to the pan.
6. Fill your pan with water so the chicken and vegetables are completely covered.
7. Add in the cider vinegar.
8. Turn the stove on High and bring to a boil.
9. Reduce the heat and let the stock simmer for about 3-4 hours.
10. Check often and top back up with water if the ingredients become uncovered.
11. Take off the heat and carefully remove the chicken, placing it to one side.
12. You now need to strain the liquid from the stockpot into another bowl using a sieve to get rid of all the lumps.
13. Leave the stock and the chicken to one side to cool.
14. Once cool, tear or cut the meat from the bones.
15. Once the stock has cooled, use immediately or place it in a sealed container and keep in the fridge for up to 3 days.

Per Serving: Calories 57, Protein 7 g, Carbohydrates 2 g, Fat 2 g, Cholesterol: 35mg, Sodium 31 mg, Potassium 126mg, Phosphorus 65 mg, Calcium: 21mg Fiber: 1g

Lime Rice with Coconut and Chili

SERVES 5 / PREP TIME: 15 MINUTES / COOK TIME: 2 HOURS

Mild, tangy and with a little bit of zest. This is a perfect base to add a little extra flavor to your favorite rice dishes.

2 tbsp. of olive oil
2 green onions, thinly sliced
1 red chilli, seeded and finely diced
1 clove of garlic, minced
2 tbsp. of unsalted butter
2 cups of white rice
1 lime, juiced
½ stick of lemon grass, finely chopped

2 bay leaves
1 cup of coconut milk (unen-riched)
2 cups of water
1 tsp. of ground black pepper

1. Preheat the slow cooker to Low.
2. Heat the oil in a wok over a high heat and add the onions, chilli and garlic.
3. Cook and for 5 minutes until the onions soften but aren't brown.
4. Add the butter and stir in the rice for 2-3 minutes to warm it through.
5. Turn the heat up to high.
6. Add in the lime, lemongrass, bay leaves, coconut milk and water.
7. Transfer everything to the slow cooker.
8. Cover it up and cook for 2 hours, stirring after the first hour.
9. Sprinkle with the ground black pepper to serve.

Per Serving: Calories: 247
Protein: 3g
Carbohydrates: 22g
Fat: 17g
Cholesterol: 0mg
Sodium: 11mg
Potassium: 194mg
Phosphorus: 82mg
Calcium: 33mg
Fiber: 2g

Roasted Beets with Lemon and Honey

SERVES 5 / PREP TIME: 5 MINUTES / COOK TIME: 6-7 HOURS

Roasting the beets brings out the sweet, mellow flavour, perfect for a side or added to other dishes.

2 tbsp. of olive oil
10 medium beets (approx. 4 pounds),
trimmed and peeled
1/3 cup of water
2 tbsp. of honey
2 tbsp. of cider vinegar
½ tsp. of garlic powder
1 lemon, juiced
A pinch of freshly ground pepper

1. Rub the inside of your slow cooker with olive oil.
2. Add the beets to the bottom of the slow cooker.
3. In a small bowl, whisk together the remaining ingredients and pour over the beets.
4. Cover and cook on Low for 6-7 hours until the beets are very soft.
5. Remove the beets from the slow cooker and slice them.
6. (Hint: You could blend these in a food processor to make a delicious puree to add to meats, fish or vegetables.)

Per Serving: Calories: 129
Protein: 2g
Carbohydrates: 20g
Fat: 6g
Cholesterol: 0mg
Sodium: 94mg
Potassium: 382mg
Phosphorus: 48mg
Calcium: 23mg
Fiber: 2g

Sweet Onion Relish

SERVES 10 / PREP TIME: 5 MINUTES / COOK TIME: 8-9 HOURS

A sweet and tangy side which goes amazingly well with barbecue food or even curries.

---

10 medium white onions, peeled and
thickly sliced
½ cup unsalted butter, diced
1 tsp. of garlic powder
A pinch of white pepper

---

1. Place the onion slices in the slow cooker and top with the butter pieces.
2. Sprinkle on the garlic powder and black pepper.
3. Cook on High for 8-9 hours until the onion is well caramelized.

Per Serving: Calories: 43.5
Protein: 0.5g
Carbohydrates: 5.5g
Fat: 2.5g
Cholesterol: 6mg
Sodium: 2mg
Potassium: 88mg
Phosphorus: 19.5mg
Calcium: 12.5mg
Fiber: 0.5g

Poached Spiced Apples and Pears

SERVES 4 / PREP TIME: 5 MINUTES / COOK TIME: 7-8 HOURS

Sweet and fragrantly spiced for a delicious dessert.

---

2 apples, peeled and halved
2 pears, peeled and halved
1 tbsp. of cloves
1 tsp. of allspice

1 cinnamon stick
1 tsp. of brown sugar

---

1. Turn the slow cooker to a low setting.
2. Peel and half the apples and pears.
3. Poke the cloves into the flesh of the fruits at even spaces.
4. Place into the slow cooker and cover with water.
5. Add the allspice, cinnamon stick and the brown sugar. Mix.
6. Cover and cook for about 7-8 hours.
7. Serve however you like.
8. (Hint: It works especially well with crumbled ginger cookies on the top.)

Per Serving: Calories: 73
Protein: 0g
Carbohydrates: 19g
Fat: 0g
Cholesterol: 0mg
Sodium: 3mg
Potassium: 138mg
Phosphorus: 17mg
Calcium: 19mg
Fiber: 4g

Honey and Mustard Glazed Root Vegetables

SERVES 5 / PREP TIME: 5 MINUTES / COOK TIME: 7-8 HOURS

Slow roasted root vegetables with a tangy sweet glaze.

4 medium carrots, peeled and roughly chopped
2 cups of rutabaga, peeled and chunked
1 tbsp. of mustard
2 tbsp. of honey
½ cup. of water
1 tbsp. of unsalted butter

A pinch of ground black pepper

1. Place all of the ingredients in the slow cooker and stir well.
2. Cover and cook on Low for 7 to 8 hours.
3. When the vegetables are tender, serve as a side or with fluffy rice.

Per Serving: Calories: 89
Protein: 1g
Carbohydrates: 17g
Fat: 3g
Cholesterol: 6mg
Sodium: 63mg
Potassium: 333mg
Phosphorus: 55mg
Calcium: 51mg
Fiber: 3g

CONVERSION TABLES

Volume

Imperial	Metric
1 tbsp	15ml
2 fl oz	55 ml
3 fl oz	75 ml
5 fl oz (¼ pint)	150 ml
10 fl oz (½ pint)	275 ml
1 pint	570 ml
1 ¼ pints	725 ml
1 ¾ pints	1 litre
2 pints	1.2 litres
2½ pints	1.5 litres
4 pints	2.25 litres

Oven temperatures

Gas Mark	Fahrenheit	Celsius
1/4	225	110
1/2	250	130
1	275	140
2	300	150
3	325	170
4	350	180
5	375	190
6	400	200
7	425	220
8	450	230
9	475	240

Weight

Imperial	Metric
½ oz	10 g
¾ oz	20 g
1 oz	25 g
1½ oz	40 g
2 oz	50 g
2½ oz	60 g
3 oz	75 g
4 oz	110 g
4½ oz	125 g
5 oz	150 g
6 oz	175 g
7 oz	200 g
8 oz	225 g
9 oz	250 g
10 oz	275 g
12 oz	350 g

REFERENCES

Garrick, R. (2008) 'Prevalence of chronic kidney disease in the United States', Yearbook of Medicine, 2008, pp. 215–217. doi: 10.1016/s0084-3873(08)79151-x.

Coresh, J., Astor, B.C., Greene, T., Eknoyan, G. and Levey, A.S. (2003) 'Prevalence of chronic kidney disease and decreased kidney function in the adult US population: Third national health and nutrition examination survey', American Journal of Kidney Diseases, 41(1), pp. 1–12. doi: 10.1053/ajkd.2003.50007.

Kopple, J.D. (2001) 'National kidney foundation K/DOQI clinical practice guidelines for nutrition in chronic renal failure', American Journal of Kidney Diseases, 37(1), pp. S66–S70. doi: 10.1053/ajkd.2001.20748.

Wilhelm-Leen, E.R., Hall, Y.N., Tamura, M.K. and Chertow, G.M. (2009) 'Frailty and chronic kidney disease: The Third national health and nutrition evaluation survey', The American Journal of Medicine, 122(7), pp. 664–671.e2. doi: 10.1016/j.amjmed.2009.01.026

Kidney Disease Outcomes Quality Initiative (K/DOQI) and the Dialysis Outcomes and Practice Patterns Study (DOPPS): Nutrition guidelines, indicators, and practices
Kalantar-Zadeh, K., Gutekunst, L., Mehrotra, R., Kovesdy, C.P., Bross, R., Shinaberger, C.S., Noori, N., Hirschberg, R., Benner, D., Nissenson, A.R. and Kopple, J.D. (2010) 'Understanding sources of dietary phosphorus in the treatment of patients with chronic kidney disease', Clinical Journal of the American Society of Nephrology, 5(3), pp. 519–530. doi: 10.2215/cjn.06080809.

Epstein, F.H., Brenner, B.M., Meyer, T.W. and Hostetter, T.H. (1982) 'Dietary protein intake and the progressive nature of kidney disease:', New England Journal of Medicine, 307(11), pp. 652–659. doi: 10.1056/nejm198209093071104.

Research, K. (2016) Kidney research UK - kidney research UK. Available at: https://www.kidneyresearchuk.org/health-information/chronic-kidney-disease (Accessed: 25 March 2016).

Foundation, N.K. (2014) Nutrition. Available at: https://www.kidney.org/nutrition (Accessed: 20 February2016).

nc, D.H.P. (2004) Top 15 healthy foods for people with kidney disease. Available at: https://www.davita.com/kidney-disease/diet-and-nutrition/lifestyle/top-15-healthy-foods-for-people-with-kidney-disease/e/5347 (Accessed: 25 July 2016).

Capicchiano, D. (2017) Top 7 tips for A healthy renal diet. Available at: http://www.kidneycoach.com/1089/renal-diet-top-7-tips-for-renal-failure/ (Accessed: 14 January 2017).

Index

Made in the USA
Columbia, SC
03 February 2019